BISHOP MORRIS BROWN

THE INVISIBLE MAN OF THE AFRICAN METHODIST EPISCOPAL CHURCH

BISHOP MORRIS BROWN

THE INVISIBLE MAN OF THE AFRICAN METHODIST EPISCOPAL CHURCH

Rev. Dr. Thomas L. Bess, Sr.
Rev. Garland D. Davis

JEWELL JORDAN PUBLISHING LLC
OKLAHOMA

Printed in the United States of America.

For information address Jewell Jordan Publishing, LLC, 1205
South Air Depot Blvd, Suite 153, Midwest City, Oklahoma 73110

Cover and Interior Photos by Raymond B. Cody
Interior Design by The Roberts Group

Library of Congress Control Number: 2019913091

ISBN: 978-0-9778418-3-7

First edition

The paper in this book meets the guidelines for permanence and
durability of the Committee on Production Guidelines for Book
Longevity of the Council of Library Resources.

THIS BOOK IS DEDICATED TO

Dr. Gretchen B. Bess, Steven Bess, Thomas Bess, Jr., Mia Bess, Dr. Virginia Manning and Retired Presiding Elder George Manning, who challenged me educationally, the many students and members who loved the African Methodist Episcopal Church, and the late Bishop F.H. Talbot who nurtured me in the early years of ministry and gave me opportunities to grow in the church.

I also want to thank the late Bishop John Hurst Adams for his support of my ministry while pastoring at Flipper Temple AME in Atlanta, Georgia; and, to all my sons and daughters in ministry.

CONTENTS

FOREWORD

The African Methodist Episcopal Church and lovers of African American history are indebted to Dr. Thomas Bess and Rev. Garland D. Davis for this informative and invaluable resource, "Bishop Morris Brown: The Invisible Man of The African Methodist Episcopal Church." For most members of the African Methodist Episcopal Church, the life, service and witness of Bishop Morris Brown is unknown. We see his name listed as the second bishop of the AME Church, we know of churches named after him, and are told that his remains are entombed with those of Bishop Richard and his wife Sarah Allen. Indeed, the title of this work is very appropriate, for Bishop Morris Brown is "the invisible man of African Methodism."

The question is why? Morris Brown, born in Charleston, South Carolina, migrated to Philadelphia, Pennsylvania where he met and collaborated with Richard Allen. From this collaboration Morris Brown became "the right arm" for Bishop Richard Allen in the newly founded AME Church. Bishop Richard Allen didn't have to do everything, because Morris Brown was by his side. Morris Brown was a man of great faith; whose religious grounding was in the Methodist Episcopal Church. His faith like Richard Allen's caused him to protest discrimination. Morris Brown was shaped by the times in which he lived, and by his faith and life he impacted those times for the better. He was prepared to assume leadership when it was thrust upon him.

Becoming the second elected and consecrated bishop of the AME Church, like a "good shepherd," he guided the church to growth numerically, and expanded the church to Kentucky, Missouri and other states. The AME Church grew larger and stronger under his leadership.

But not only was Morris Brown a great churchman, but he was also an extraordinary human rights activist, champion of social justice and a prophetic leader. It is not accurate or right that African American history be written without including the contribution of Bishop Morris Brown. Of note is Morris Brown's relationship and support of the efforts of Denmark Vesey. While both came from different backgrounds, they managed to overcome their differences to promote freedom for slaves and advancement of Black people. Morris Brown put his neck on the line in the struggle to free Blacks. Ultimately it was the alleged relationship with Denmark Vesey that caused Brown's church in Charleston to be closed and forced him to flee to Philadelphia.

It was Morris Brown's willingness to go to jail, and to risk his life to protest the city of Charleston's crackdown on Black churches that caused Richard Allen to admire and make Morris Brown one of his confidants, and eventually the second bishop of the African Methodist Episcopal Church. Bishop Morris Brown had an extraordinary ministry as a bishop in the African Methodist Episcopal Church. While not well learned himself, he encouraged and mentored others to get as much education as they could, including Daniel Payne, who himself would later become a bishop in the church, and is considered one of the "Four Horsemen" of the AME Church. During his episcopacy, Bishop Morris Brown expanded the AME Church to six conferences, 62 elders, 300 churches and more than

17,000 members. It is important to note the time in which this was achieved, a difficult and threatening time. The work of Bishop Morris Brown laid the foundation that others would build upon, notably, Daniel Payne, Paul Quinn and Henry McNeal Turner, all of whom became bishops in the AME Church, and along with Bishop Allen, the Four Horsemen of the AME Church. The life, labor and witness of Bishop Morris Brown should cause the Four Horsemen to become the "Five Horsemen" of the AME Church. A champion of freedom and social justice, one who risked his own life for the sake of Black freedom and the survival and freedom of the Black Church, a confidant and "right arm" of Bishop Richard Allen, one who led the expansion of the AME Church, and mentored the church's future leaders, Morris Brown, "the invisible man", has earned and deserves to no longer be "invisible." The work he has done speaks well and loud for him.

Thanks is due to Dr. Thomas Bess and Rev. Garland D. Davis for this invaluable contribution to the history of not only the African Methodist Episcopal Church, but to African American history. We are deeply indebted to them for unveiling one of the great heroes of the faith, whose efforts continue to bless the African Methodist Episcopal Church, and which continues to inspire many of us in the ongoing struggle for freedom and justice.

Bishop Reginald T. Jackson
Sixth Episcopal District
African Methodist Episcopal Church

INTRODUCTION

While working at the Interdenominational Theological Center (ITC) in Atlanta, Georgia as an Adjunct Professor of African Methodist Episcopal (AME) History and Polity, it became abundantly clear to me that during a critical time in the life of the AME Church God had prepared a man first in Charleston, South Carolina and later Philadelphia, Pennsylvania to take the reins of the AME denomination after the founder's death and propelling it to a place in modern history. Bishop Morris Brown of Charleston, South Carolina made many contributions to the civil rights of African people, the abolitionist movement, and the insurrection conspiracy led by Denmark Vesey; however, his major influence on the AME Church is largely unknown.

Unlike historical figures such as Frederick Douglass, Booker T. Washington, W. E. B. DuBois, and even Richard Allen, Brown never felt compelled to write his autobiography, thus leaving very little information about his overall background and only a glimpse into his personality. Yet, his contribution to the AME Church was immeasurable as he was responsible for major growth of the denomination in certain American colonies as well as in Canada. His aid to the AME founder, Richard Allen, in conjunction with his role in the AME Church, contributed to his consecration as bishop in the AME Church. As the second elected and consecrated bishop in the AME Church, he not only took the church forward, he expanded the church into Missouri, Kentucky, and other southwestern states. Bishop Morris Brown was the steady hand that God groomed for the moment to carry the church forward. Yet when AME leaders are lifted, such as the Four Horsemen—Richard Allen, Henry McNeal Turner, Paul Quinn, and Daniel Payne—whose exceptional work advanced, developed and strengthened the church, Bishop Morris Brown is left standing in the shadow of history.

The story of Morris Brown, the man, is a discussion that is relative to the many nuances associated with the black experience in America. It is a discussion of a people who were dehumanized, used, abused, and made to submit or face death. This is also a conversation about a people who fought and rebelled against their lives of servitude and the poor conditions under which they lived and functioned.

This conversation about the second bishop of African Methodism is one that would be irrelevant without the discussion of Charleston, South Carolina and the pivotal role that city played in the large number of African Americans whose ancestors from West Africa entered the United States at Charleston as part of the slave trade. Ultimately, it is a conversation about one man who was born within the first 100 years of America's existence, during colonization, and born in a location that affected the entire infrastructure of a nation.

The profound contribution that Morris Brown has made to the African Methodist Episcopal Church, to the abolitionist movement, to the legacy of Charleston, South Carolina, and to the fabric of American history has been overshadowed by the focus on others with similar goals and objectives. He is an unsung hero, not only in U.S. history, but ironically in the history of African Methodism and African American history. Thus, the purpose of this book is to inform, acknowledge, and honor a man who made great sacrifices and wielded considerable influence in both the abolitionist fight and the building of AME churches.

Possessed of a tall, corpulent frame, Morris Brown had a great impact on other races in many aspects of his life. Raised in the local Methodist Episcopal Church, Brown found favor among white men. Yet, he also had common ground with the Africans, slave and free, in his birthplace of Charleston, South Carolina. Brown was a rebel and vigilant in his fight against the many injustices that he witnessed, which were suffered by his African brothers and sisters at the hands of white men. Brown's legacy is rich and lives on in the many mid-Atlantic and Canadian African Methodist churches that still exist today. His legacy is found in the determination to survive of many who came after him. He was a courageous man who lived his life selflessly and blamelessly.

What we do know for certain is that while free Africans did exist during the late 18th century, they were in many ways still living as bondservants, not being allowed to experience the same liberties of the white man. Freedoms and liberties such as these included suffrage rights, serving as a witness in a court of law, and the right to receive an education. It was almost as if the African freeman had no purpose or direction. This way of life was especially true in colonial Charleston, South Carolina. Yet, they were able to grow and become influential decision makers.

We invite you to explore the heroic, humble, godly, Christian preacher, Morris Brown—whose life had favor—and the effect that Bishop Brown had on the AME church essentially caused by the events surrounding the insurrection led by

Denmark Vesey that resulted in Brown's banishment from Charleston and the great impression he had on Richard Allen.

Dr. Thomas Bess
August 2019

CHAPTER I

MORRIS BROWN— EARLY AND FAMILY LIFE

What Morris Brown was able to achieve in his life is matched by few of his contemporaries considering he was a free Black man who grew up in Charleston, South Carolina.

Morris Brown was born on February 13, 1770. His family was part of a sizeable black population in the city of Charleston where most Africans were enslaved. In the year of Brown's birth, more than 5,800 enslaved blacks and 24 free blacks resided in the city, compared to a total of 5,030 whites. "Within this city where blacks were the majority, Brown's family circulated within [a free black community], whose members were often so closely related to aristocratic whites in the city that they were exempt from the racist restrictions imposed on all enslaved people."[1]

Charleston was the largest and most active slave port in North America and the hub of the African slave trade in the south at the time of Morris Brown's birth. The city of Charleston was founded and settled by English colonists in 1670, growing from a colonial seaport to a wealthy city by the mid-eighteenth century. The comparatively small, mainly commercial cities of the south like Charleston contained a substantial black population. Given these characteristics along with the south's racial ideology and the heritage of slavery, we might expect the black communities such as these in the south to have had experiences which were comparatively unique. Thus, no comprehensive view of blacks in the south would be complete without considering blacks in the pivotal city of Charleston.

At the height of the slave trade, Charleston was more densely populated by Africans than the white population. Being close to the Atlantic Ocean, Charleston Harbor served as the gateway for African slaves to entire the United States to be bought and sold by harsh slave traders. Hence, a large percentage of Africans in Charleston were slaves tending to South Carolina's agricultural needs, particularly their rice fields. White slave owners found that it was more economically sound to buy slaves than to hire field hands who would require a daily, weekly or monthly wage.

By the end of the antebellum period, the city of Charleston declined in relative importance as its commercial preeminence fell victim to the southwestward spread of the cotton kingdom and the rivalry of the emerging southern river towns which profited from the steamboat trade. Despite its economic misfortunes, Charleston maintained an atmosphere of gentility because of its location in the heart of the South Carolina Lowcountry. Life in Charleston for free blacks was less rigid socially than the remainder of the state. Charleston was considered an attractive city because it provided economic potential for "free persons of color." However, during the period of 1830-1865, blacks in South Carolina were met with hostility from most whites; and therefore, the status of free blacks was almost the same as that of the slaves.

By 1850, blacks had outnumbered whites in seven of the eight previous decades. However, the primary obstacles created by whites to impede the growth of free blacks were legislative acts designed to prohibit the emancipation of slaves and the entrance of free persons of color into South Carolina from other states and counties. The white citizens were constantly petitioning the state legislature for additional restrictive acts and amendments to those already in force, which would serve to prevent the population of free blacks from becoming too large. Hence, South Carolina's Slave Code of 1740, was a series of laws aimed at controlling the population of enslaved African Americans. It prohibited slaves from gathering without white supervision, learning to read and write, and growing their own food. The legislation was enacted shortly after the Stono Rebellion, which reinforced slave owners' fears of slave uprisings. The Stono Rebellion was a slave rebellion that began in September of 1739. It was the largest slave uprising near the Stono River southwest of Charleston where some two dozen slaves gathered seeking liberty. After raiding a firearms shop, the group head south towards Spanish Florida—a refuge for escapees—with their numbers swelling to approximately 80. In the end the slaves were defeated; the death toll included more than 25 white people and 35 to 50 African slaves.[2]

The ensuing anti-literacy laws prohibited anyone from providing instruction in reading or writing to any black person, whether slave or free. Even providing religious education and instruction was discouraged for fear that more than religious education would be provided. Despite Morris Brown being part of the city's black elite, because of these laws, he did not receive a formal education.

The discussion of young Morris Brown becomes a historical reference that begins in America's colonial times that led up to the Revolutionary War. The year of Morris Brown's birth (1770), whites were a minority in Charleston. According to the 1790 census, Charleston was home to 15,402 whites and 51,585 blacks.[3] Less than ten percent of the population controlled most of the wealth and political power. Charleston had a larger African population than New York, Boston and Philadelphia combined. That reality demanded that the city and the activities of the people be controlled by the government with the help of a police force.

A large group of free blacks were the mulatto offspring of their masters and slave women. Therefore, free blacks in Charleston were frequently called free persons of color. Free blacks were slaves who had either purchased their freedom or were emancipated by their owners. Other free blacks migrated to Charleston. By the time Brown was twenty years old, there were about 775 free blacks in Charleston.

Morris Brown was raised during some pivotal times in American history. The colonization of both northern and southern states was underway as America drew closer to becoming the United States of America. During his formative years, Brown must have witnessed the effect of the Revolutionary War that began in 1775 and lasted until the time that American colonies gained their independence in 1783. It was amid this era that the Freed African Society was being born and African Methodism began with Richard Allen, Absalom Jones, and others on the front lines in its establishment in 1787.

Morris Brown received Christ's salvation at an early age with his conversion to Methodism. Brown grew in the Methodist Episcopal (ME) church, and was soon licensed to preach. African slaves were free to go to church and worship in the ME Church. The ME Church in South Carolina was filled with Africans because of the abolitionist stand that they took. As their numbers grew, both generally and within the African Church in Charleston, Brown emerged as their leader.

Later Brown became an ordained deacon and an itinerant elder making his way to Philadelphia and back to Charleston to make his connection with Richard Allen and the newly organized African Methodist Episcopal Church. He would eventually become an influential leader in the community among blacks and whites in Charleston, South Carolina, and ultimately a great builder of AME Churches in several states and in Canada.

Most people knew Brown as a religious leader, minister of the gospel and eventually the nation's second bishop of the AME Church. Brown's doctrine revolved around two beliefs: Christian moralism and liberation. Brown believed that Christian religion defined the essential elements of daily life. As a husband and father, he was affectionate, watchful and wise; always setting an example that pointed them to the "Lamb of God which taketh away the sins of the world."[4] As a friend, he was faithful to a fault. As a man of God, he treated all men as if they were brothers. There was no doubt that he was a good man, a caring father, a fair man, and a disciple of the Lord. He was an upright man with a respectable reputation. He had good morals and character. Brown earned a reputation for helping those who were less fortunate by assisting slaves to purchase their freedom while also teaching and advising both free and enslaved Africans in the region and operating a prosperous business as a bootmaker and shoe repairman.

Although there were exclusive organizations within the African community in Charleston, such as the Brown Fellowship Society—which initially only welcomed light-skinned blacks in order to gain favor with whites in Charleston[5]—to which Brown could have belonged, it is unlikely he either participated in or approved of such restrictive organizations as to do so would have been inconsistent with the actions he took in contributing to the spiritual and civil needs of all black people in his commune. The exclusivity of these organizations was almost as demeaning as the inhumane treatment that black Africans were already experiencing. The fact that Brown was able to choose between a life of privilege and that of struggle, was compelling. This is awe-inspiring and reminiscent to the life of Moses found in the book of Exodus of the Bible. As Moses was compelled to be God's vessel in freeing the children of Israel, Morris Brown seemed compelled to lead Charleston's Africans to the liberation of worshipping the one, true God Almighty.

Although unschooled, Brown was an advocate for education. His inability to read or write did not inhibit his success as a businessman—he was shoemaker—and as a profound leader, able to build many congregations and one whom many would follow.

In 1800, Brown married a woman named Bella who was enslaved. Because Bella was a slave, all six of their children were born slaves—Malcom, Morris Jr, John, Samuel, Martha and Charlotte. Free blacks could file petitions to the South Carolina Legislature to request permission to free members of their family who had been purchased from their former slave owners. After years of laboring and saving, Brown bought his wife and children from Hannah LeSense for 650 pounds.

Having purchased his family, Brown continued to use his earnings to liberate other Charleston slaves; but because of his efforts to do so he later served twelve months in the city's Workhouse. The first Workhouse was a former sugar warehouse—which led to an odd euphemism created by white masters who would threaten their slaves with being sent "for a little sugar" if bad behavior continued.[6] "Getting sugar" meant being flogged and walking the treadmill. Slaves walked on the treadmill in shifts, providing power for grinding corn. If an exhausted slave tripped and fell on the ever-moving treadmill, he often would lose a foot or leg between the rollers. Overseers used rawhide whips to maintain order because it flayed the skin and bruised the muscle tissue beneath the skin. In order to help free his people from such heinous treatment, Brown used his business and the church to help slaves escape north to freedom. Brown believed in nonviolence but confronted reform.

In 1818, following the actions of whites seeking to maintain control of Charleston's Africans—free and enslaved—Brown would leave the predominantly white but racially segregated Methodist Church in Charleston in protest against discrimination. More than 4,000 black members of the white churches in the city followed Brown to his new church, the African Church of Charleston.

OLD BETHEL
METHODIST CHURCH

CHAPTER II

BIRTH OF THE AFRICAN CHURCH IN CHARLESTON, SOUTH CAROLINA

Morris Brown worked tirelessly to forge an independent African Methodist Church in Charleston. In 1816, Brown, along with former slave Henry Drayton, sailed to Philadelphia to confer with Richard Allen of the Bethel Church. They arrived in the city shortly after the organizing of the African Methodist Episcopal church.[7]

Brown and Drayton returned to Charleston in 1817 to discover that Anthony Senter the leader of a group of white members of the Methodist Church who no longer identified themselves as "friends" to the Africans nor to abolitionism was reasserting control over the majority Black members, including the disbursement of their collection plates and revenues. Trustees of Bethel, led by Senter, decided to build a hearse house atop a small black cemetery adjoining the Bethel Methodist Church.[8] Africans had a special allegiance to the dead—believing that graveyards should never be disturbed. All graves seemed to represent marginal property—land which was not likely to be used for any other purpose. The burial spots were often described as "ragged patches of live-oak and palmetto and brier tangle which gives a sign that there are graves within,—graves scattered without symmetry, and often without headstones or head-boards, or sticks."[9] Therefore, African members of the church were so upset by this decision to build atop a cemetery followed by their loss of control over church affairs that they decided to leave the church in protest to begin construction of an independent African Church in another location.

When thousands of Africans left the ME church after this gross display of disdain and disrespect by whites in the ME church, former African church members formed three different AME organizations that would eventually be called the Bethel Circuit. Of the three newly formed Methodist organizations, Morris Brown was placed in the position of leadership and founded the African Church of Charleston in 1817.

In 1818, Brown traveled to Philadelphia and was admitted as an Itinerant Elder in the AME Church. His Charleston church, which had grown to more than 3,000 members by 1822, affiliated with this northern black denomination.

Built on Anson Street near the corner of Boundary (this corner still exists today), Charleston's African Methodist congregation grew quickly and as a result, the city's black community began work on a second church on Cow Alley (now Philadelphia Street) in a predominately black Hampstead neighborhood along the town's northern edge which later became part of the Bethel Circuit. The African Church's membership was made up of free black artisans.

Having been ordained by Bishop Richard Allen in Philadelphia, Brown was named pastor of the new congregation.

Brown was a pragmatist who believed that his main responsibility was to protect his flock and preserve their sense of hope for the future. Since white authorities were always threatening to close the doors of the church at any moment, Brown walked a thin line between giving the people hope and keeping the doors open. Worshipping under these circumstances forced Brown to surrender the principle of political leadership— giving up on the will-to-power and taking no immediate action—in hopes of keeping the doors open. Many of the slaves appreciated Brown's position; but the more radical members regarded him as a good man who could not be trusted.

Brown's fair-skin and his son's membership in the Brown Fellowship Society contributed to the more radical church members' mistrust of Brown. The Brown Fellowship Society was a club for those who considered themselves "brown" mulattos, an important distinction at the time when society in Charleston recognized three races: White, Mulatto, and Negro. The only dark-complexioned men that were allowed into the Society had straight hair, which signified a white blood line despite their dark skin. The rest of the black population was ignored by the Brown Fellowship Society for the sake of gaining the support of the white population.

Brown did not choose this type of society to become who he was. He was an advocate for all black people; and was more concerned about their eternal destinations than their burial plots.

However, because of the persistent fears by white society that an African Methodist leader would appear as a latter-day Moses, Morris Brown's eloquent sermons did not deliver a theology of liberation. His primary message to blacks was that all Christians were equal in the sight of God, a message that provided hope and sustenance to the slaves. For Brown to preach liberation in an oppressed environment would only heighten the fear of white owners that the slaves would ultimately plot rebellion against them.

The white churches preached a message of strict obedience and insisted on slave attendance at white-controlled churches. Many blacks saw these white churches, in which ministers promoted obedience to one's master as the highest religious ideal, as a mockery of the "true" Christian message of equality and liberation as they knew it.[10] Rev. Brown, whose allegiance was to the black community, believed that his first responsibility was to protect his black flock and preserve their sense of hope for the future. As a result, blacks organized their own invisible institution through signals, passwords and messages not discernible to whites. White authorities made daily threats to close Brown's church, which is to say that they threatened to close the focus of black cultural and social life in Charleston.

Historically, the black church has been a place for creating individual, systemic, and political change within the black community. Since its emergence in the 18th century, the black church has served as a safe haven for blacks—a place to worship God together, and a place where blacks are motivated to rebuild their communities. The black church stood in the eye of the white-supremacist storm. Instead of falling apart, the black church practically willed itself to exponential growth through political self-determination, community outreach and organizing that made it the most important black institution America has ever produced. So, to threaten to close a black church was not simply closing a place of worship but an elimination of black community and social change.

CHAPTER III

DENMARK VESEY REVOLT AND THE CLOSING OF THE AME CHURCH

B rown's congregation understood that he put the church over any one individual. However, there was a member of the African Church at Hampstead who did have a clear theology of liberation. His name was Denmark Vesey. He was a Class Leader and lay preacher in the Church. Vesey preached from two primary passages of the Bible:

> Joshua 6:21, *They utterly destroyed everything in the city, both man and woman, young and old, and ox and sheep and donkey, with the edge of the sword.*

> And

> Zechariah 14:1-2, *Behold, a day is coming for the Lord when the spoil taken from you will be divided among you. For I will gather all the nations against Jerusalem to battle, and the city will be captured, the houses plundered, the women ravished and half the city exiled, but the rest of the people will not be cut off from the city.*[11]

This latter verse from the Book of Zechariah was one of Vesey's favorite scriptures in the Bible. Vesey took the Word literally—to destroy the city by fire. When God instructed his leaders to destroy all, Vesey saw that as an opportunity to physically destroy by killing everyone and burning the city so they would not be a threat to their escape.

Denmark Vesey, also known as Telemarque in his early years, was born around 1767 on the island of St. Thomas. Others have speculated that he was born in Africa and later sold to St. Thomas.[12] It was on the island of St. Thomas that Denmark formed some of his radical views about mulattos. As a young person Vesey observed how mulattos always sided with the master class and even served as police whenever a slave revolt arose. What he witnessed in St. Thomas shaped his viewpoint.

When Denmark was sixteen years old, he was sold to Captain Josey Vesey who was transporting 390 slaves from St. Thomas to the French St. Dominique, later the Republic of Haiti. Because the Captain found Telemarque (Denmark) beautiful and intelligent, he was allowed to help out on the deck and was later given better clothes to wear. The captain and crew treated Telemarque as something of an indulged pet. Telemarque's world changed when they arrived in St. Dominique where he was put in chains and sold with the rest of the slaves. He was headed for an early death in the cane fields of St. Dominique. Telemarque took his own fate into his hands by faking an epileptic seizure, causing him to be sold back to Captain Vesey because he was considered damaged property. The island doctor certified Telemarque's illness as a justified reason for him to be considered damaged property. Captain Vesey later realized that Denmark's supposed epilepsy and foaming at the mouth was a charade, but he never tried to sell him again. Instead, Denmark traveled the world on the slave ship and learned the culture of many tribes and spoke the language. He spoke French with fluency. He also saw the ugly slave trade up close when Captain Vesey settled in Charleston.[13]

Although Denmark was Vesey's right-hand man in the office and with the slaves, he was respected by the slave community. In 1800, after seventeen years as a slave in Charleston, Vesey purchased a lottery ticket. Denmark won $1500 and bought his freedom for $600 from Captain Joseph Vesey. He used the remaining $900 to become a carpenter. He became a respected member of the Charleston community and joined the Second Presbyterian Church. He began his second decade of freedom by becoming a member of the African Methodist Episcopal Church.

Denmark became a messianic believer who publicly spoke out against black slavery. During Vesey's life in Charleston, he had multiple wives and children. Most of his family were slaves and one of his life's frustration was his inability to buy their freedom. One of his sons, Robert Vesey was free and became a successful builder in the city. It was in Denmark's second decade of freedom that he became radicalized and literally sought to carry out the mandate of the scriptures. He used his position as Class Leader and Lay Preacher in the AME church to push his messianic message in a way that opened the minds of the slaves.

During this time, questions were raised about Morris Brown's knowledge of what Denmark was teaching in his church. Although Vesey saw Brown as a pious and good man, he felt that Brown could not be totally trusted. Sunday was the black community's day of services, rest and visitations. Lay clergy conducted nightly "Class Meetings" during the work week in a retired building or private home. White authorities routinely sat in rear pews during Brown's formal sermons, but typically no white person attended the nightly sessions. Each Class had a black preacher or leader who was chosen by the church hierarchy. If Vesey felt that Brown and Henry Drayton were being compliant to the white authority, he failed to recognize Brown's contempt or simply felt that the aging bootmaker was too important to be ignored. Vesey continued to preach his gospel of liberty and hate. If Brown's Sunday sermons included a creative mixing of African and Christian elements, Vesey's twilight teachings were different.

In June 1818, AME representatives from the parent church in Philadelphia arrived in Charleston. Area whites trusted Brown, but envoys of Richard Allen's northern church were another matter. On Sunday, June 7th, the city guard rushed into the church and arrested 140 free negroes and slaves, one of them was presumed to be Denmark Vesey. Charleston and Philadelphia blacks were released the following morning by the city magistrates. Black ministers appeared before the City Council to request permission to hold meetings but were not approved. The Philadelphia church men were determined to carry on, so they organized another large service. Once again, the city guard arrested the congregation.[14]

In later years, Morris Brown was always silent about Denmark and his connection to him; however, Brown did enjoy his public connection with Vesey. What Vesey and Brown shared was their dislike of slavery. Morris Brown worked tirelessly to keep the doors of the church open because the white community feared blacks worshipping on their own. White leaders in this southern city along with slave owners across the south were criticized for keeping slaves in spiritual ignorance. It was a delicate balance between freedom to worship and closing the church. In the years 1817 and 1818, the city government sent its police force to beat and arrest the AME members and to destroy their property. In December 1817, 469 members were arrested and charged with disorderly conduct.

Thus, June of 1818 proved to be the last straw. *The Courier* newspaper reported that "153 negroes and slaves, belonging to the African Church, were arrested and taken to the Guard House. The City Council sentenced five of them, consisting of a bishop and four ministers to a one-month prison sentence or give security to leave the state. Several received lashes and/or paid a fine."[15] Vesey was purported to be one of the ones who received ten lashes. Rev. Morris Brown was ordered to leave the state, but he chose to spend a month in the Workhouse. The armed assault on the African Church discouraged many congregants and forced Morris Brown to be more cautious unless he wanted to be fined or whipped.

Blacks continued to hold late night services despite warnings. In 1820, several blacks were arrested for holding a late-night service on Anson Street and on January 15, 1821, Councilman John J. Lafar warned Morris Brown that the city would not tolerate class leaders conducting instructional schools for slaves because this was forbidden by law. However, they tried it again. On occasion, Vesey and the other class leaders conducted their lessons in the church. To avoid those spying on the night watch, church leaders held meetings in their homes. Morris Brown with the assistance lent by Henry Drayton, Charles Carr, Amos Cruickshank, Marcus Brown and the volatile Denmark Vesey made the church the rallying point for most of Charleston's black populace.

Vesey was convinced that the same God who instructed him did not speak to the other AME leadership. He cautioned his disciples not to tell Morris Brown, Henry Drayton or Charles Carr of their plan. Rev. Brown's chief concerns included saving souls and maintaining his church as a vital black center of community life. Brown respected Vesey enough to assign him as Class leader, but the compliment was not returned. Monday Gell, scribe for the movement and another of Vesey's confidants, felt that Brown would betray them to the white authorities for the price of protecting his church. Beyond their common concern for Charleston's enslaved community, Brown and Vesey shared few opinions on how to deal with southern racism. Brown remained a loyal Christian while Vesey had long lost patience with a theology that told him to love his oppressor. Brown tried to appease white authority with his moderation, whereas Vesey had grown more combative and accepting of violence. Although Brown was a proponent of black autonomy, he also had white friends who helped him to escape the Vesey revolt.

In 1822, Denmark Vesey planned one of the largest slave revolts in the history of North America by convincing thousands of slaves that armed rebellion was their only hope for freedom. The planning of the destruction of Charleston became real when Denmark decided to gather his most trusted friends who would help put the plan together: Gullah Jack, Blind Phillip and Peter Poyas.

Gullah Jack Prichard, an East African priest, was perhaps the conspiracy's most important leader next to Vesey. Also known as Cooter Jack, he had a multidimensional role in the conspiracy. Vesey's theology of liberation, combined with Gullah Jack's African mysticism, inspired potential participants. Gullah Jack, a native of Angola, was believed to be that little man who could not be killed. His skill as an herbalist allowed him to prepare medicine for the sick and poison for the enemy. The slaves believed that with Gullah Jack amulets, the white man's bullets would not hurt or kill them.[16]

The specific plans of the insurrection were for the African slaves and freeman together, to revolt against their slave masters, to annihilate them and then flee the state of South Carolina. Tens of thousands of slaves were secretly uniting for this event. This was significant because during these times, it was against state law for slaves to enter or exit the state of South Carolina. Vesey had organized his plans with such precision that his Haitian connections were ready for a great fleet of Africans to enter Haiti for the purpose of building it up, establishing a strong economy, and starting a new life for generations to come.[17]

Denmark Vesey was described by his acquaintances as eccentric, polygamist, ambitious, domineering, mean, tough, and intolerant of human weaknesses. They said he walked the streets as if he was the only freeman in the country. He was very intelligent and a proud man. He was an unlikely candidate to unite slaves and free Black people to fight for their liberty. Vesey was constantly engaged in trying to poison the minds of the colored population against whites.

Vesey continued his use of scriptural texts to win supporters for the insurrection. He spent hours studying the Bible, eventually concluding that he had a religious duty to incite slaves to rebellion. Vesey expected aid from England and Haiti and believed that all slaves would rise in his support. He planned long and carefully for over five years. He recruited at local congregations, urging slaves to behave proudly and quoting the Bible to persuade them that acquiescence in bondage was sinful. His objective was for slaves to attempt their emancipation, however shocking and bloody might be the consequences. He believed that such efforts would be pleasing to God. One conspirator confessed that Vesey "read in the Bible where God commanded, that all should be cut off, both men and women and children, and said . . . 'it was no sin for us to do so, for the Lord had commanded us to do it.'" When someone objected to Denmark's vision of a violent revolution, his reply would be "The Lord has commanded it." He read his Bible and found in it that slavery was wrong. According to one deposition against Vesey, "His general conversation was about religion which he would apply to slavery, as for instance, he would speak of the creation of the world, in which he would say all men had equal rights, blacks as well as whites; all of his religious remarks were mingled with slavery."[18]

It was said that the Vesey Conspiracy had the best of religious worlds, the doctrinal sanction of scripture, and the practical protection of charm. In addition to bible passages from the books of Joshua and Zachariah, Vesey emphasized *Colossians 4:1: Masters, give unto your servant that which is just and equal; knowing that ye also have a Master in heaven, and Exodus 2:23-24: . . . and the children of Israel sighed by reason of the bondage, and they cried, and their cry came up onto the God by reason of the bondage.*

Dissatisfied with his second-class status as a freeman and determined to help relieve the far more oppressive conditions of the bondsmen he knew; Vesey planned and organized an uprising of city and plantation blacks. The plan reportedly called for the rebels to attack guardhouses and arsenals, seize their arms, kill all whites, burn and destroy the city, and free the slaves. As many as 9,000 blacks may have been involved. He was assisted by three close friends, the previously mentioned Gullah Jack, Blind Phillip, and Peter Poyas.

Gullah Jack provided the insurgents with trinkets that would make them invincible. In preparation for the rebellion, the combatants had to fast on parched corn and peanuts before receiving a charm from Gullah Jack that consisted of a cullah, or crab claw. On the morning of the planned uprising, the rebels were to place the crab claws in their mouths. According to Gullah Jack, this would make them invulnerable.

Gullah Jack was one of the most important recruiters in the conspiracy, due primarily to his influence over fellow slaves. Feared by others because of his abilities, this "little man who can't be killed, shot or taken" was well respected in Charleston and in the surrounding countryside. Fear reinforced Jack's threat to injure any informant who betrayed the conspiracy. After Jack was captured by local authorities, one slave was witnessed literally begging the court to send him out of state because he considered his life "in great danger from having given testimony". This witness concluded his testimony by stating "I was afraid of Gullah Jack as a conjurer." Both American and African born slaves believed in his powers. Gullah Jack combined membership in the African Methodist Church with the practice of conjure or what we call today "magic."

Before the revolt, Vesey called a meeting in which he was said to have excluded slaves who had received gifts of old coats from their masters and the pastor in charge of the African Church—Morris Brown. He excluded the slaves who were attached to their masters for obvious reasons. He excluded the pastor because he did not trust him. The famous plot involved six class leaders from Brown's AME community, ending in 131 arrests and 35 executions.

The original attack date was set for the second Sunday in July of 1822 but had to be moved forward after two conspirators were arrested on May 30th. The Class System of the independent African Methodist Association of Charleston was used as a recruiting and indoctrination vehicle as well as a communication network for the revolt. After a heavy recruitment period, Denmark had several chief lieutenants, each of whom had hundreds, if not thousands of followers who were willing to be led in a violent rebellion. The uprising of slaves in Charleston in 1822, led by Denmark Vesey and Gullah Jack was discovered by the authorities of the state and the city who deemed it wise to suppress all assemblages of free colored people and slaves. Thus, African Methodism in South Carolina was silenced in its infancy.

One of Vesey's followers, William Paul, attempted to convince Peter Devaney (also identified as Peter Desverney and Peter Prioleau), who was a house slave of a Colonel Prioleau, to participate with them in the slave revolt. However, Devany consulted William Penceel, a Brown Fellowship Society member, who instructed Devany to tell his master—who was out of town at the time—of the planned rebellion, which he later did. As the word of Vesey's plans spread, Charleston's white community, with assistance from some portions of the mulatto community, sought to undermine those plans. Vesey and others were arrested; and ultimately Vesey and some of those arrested with him were later executed.[19]

For his betrayal of Vesey, Devany was rewarded with emancipation and a lifetime pension said to be $50 per year, which was later upon his request increased to $75 per year. After gaining his freedom, Devany became a slaveowner, buying and selling slaves. For his part, William Penceel—whose advise to Devany was met with approval from the Brown Fellowship Society—was given $1000 and exempted from ever again paying the "free Negro capitation charge" imposed on all other free Africans and mulattos in Charleston. In fact, in addition to his stature among white Charlestonians, Penceel was held in high regard by the mulattos—despite the fact that free Africans and mulattos continued to be subjected to oppressive restrictions by the white power structure.[20]

Since Morris Brown was a member of the new independent Black church, he was considered a secret counselor of the group. Suspected of knowing about Vesey's plan—although there was no direct evidence of such knowledge—his white friends warned him against remaining in the state and concealed him aboard a ship leaving for Philadelphia. Before the year ended, he went north. When he returned, he was forced to leave the state and the church was forced to close. Brown's Christian attitude spoke volumes about his character because he felt that taking revenge would lead him and his oppressors to spiritual ruin. Rev. Morris Brown was implicated in the plot but was never convicted. Vesey was betrayed by one of his men and was captured and sentenced. While Denmark Vesey was in prison, he reportedly called out to his fellow prisoners in the Guard House to "Die like a man!"

Between June 19 and August 6, 1822, the Charleston Court of Magistrates and Freeholders, interrogated, tortured, and tried in closed sessions over 100 African Americans as co-conspirators. None of the religious leaders who were associated with Morris Brown were implicated in the uprising. The court sent 35 of them to the gallows, two died in custody, and nearly 40 were transported out of the United States. Instead of using gallows, they tossed ropes over an old wall known as the "Lines" built in the Northern part of Charleston. A crude platform was built for them to stand on, but the platform was built so low to the ground that when the slave fell, their necks did not break; instead they slowly strangled to death. The captain of the guards rolled down the lines, shooting each of them in the head, reloading as he went from man to man. The bodies of the convicted were given to the Medical College of South Carolina for dissection as a warning. In the aftermath, Brown and the African Church came under investigation because of the Denmark Vesey-led slave uprising in Charleston. Having arrested, tried, convicted, whipped, banished and lynched hundreds of alleged participants a white mob tore down the African Church brick by brick and set it on fire, burning it to the ground.[21]

In history, no two great men are alike. Morris Brown was a good man sometimes eloquent but not always persuasive in his sermons. Denmark Vesey was known as the eradicator of the white race. Based on their childhood and class issues, educational opportunities, and level of household comfort, it is evident where their beliefs were grounded. Brown's parents were part of the elite, so he enjoyed some great things that life had to offer. On the other hand, Vesey's upbringing was not so privileged. Morris Brown was focused on equality, the goodness of the man and the capability to do good. Vesey's view of the world was tainted with anger, bitterness and the desire to get revenge on those who treated him and the slave and black population unfairly. When Vesey's plot to lead a slave uprising was uncovered in 1822, accusations surfaced that sought to connect Brown to the conspiracy even though he was out of town when the revolt was uncovered. His safety was threatened because of the assumption that he was a co-conspirator. With the help of a white lawyer and politician, James Hamilton, Jr, he was able to flee to safety. Fearing implication, Brown fled to Philadelphia.

Early in 1823, Rev. Morris Brown, his wife Bella, and their two sons left the south and settled in Philadelphia where he served as an assistant at the Mother Bethel AME Church and as an aide to the aging Bishop Allen. At that time, the Lombard Street race riot in Philadelphia occurred near Mother Bethel Church, confirming the uneasy state of race relations in the City of Brotherly Love, but fortunately sparing the church building.

Richard Allen, the founder of the AME Church and its first bishop, gave Brown refuge and made him his assistant. Brown subsequently joined the AME circuit and began to preach and travel with his counterparts, building up the church and spreading God's Word.

Meanwhile the congregation in Charleston rebuilt the African Church and worshiped there until 1834, when the city banned all African American churches.

CHAPTER IV

MORRIS BROWN JOINS RICHARD ALLEN AT BETHEL AME CHURCH IN PHILADELPHIA, PENNSYLVANIA

Morris Brown was formally named Mother Bethel's assistant pastor, and later the assistant bishop. Richard Allen had a reputation of drawing black leaders from hundreds of miles away. Thus, upon arrival in Philadelphia, Allen and the members of Mother Bethel welcomed hundreds of former Charleston AME members. No sooner had Brown arrived in Philadelphia than Bishop Allen made sure he had a spiritual home and literal home.

At an October 2, 1822 meeting of Bethel Trustees at Allen's Spruce Street house, AME fathers guaranteed to pay "the board of Reverend Brown and such ministers and preachers as shall board with him thereafter."[22] By October 15th, Brown appeared on the Board of Trustees alongside Allen. Morris Brown quickly became Allen's confidant. Allen admired Brown for his willingness to go to jail to protest Charleston's crackdown on the free black church.

The number of AME churches had increased drastically since its organization in 1816, so Bishop Allen addressed the Baltimore Conference about the necessity of conducting the business of the church. The work of the church was increasing, which resulted in the increased importance of the business to be transacted; thus, an assistant to the bishop was deemed in order. The Baltimore Conference had a motion to create a committee of three traveling preachers to nominate two or three candidates for that position. The committee consisted of Jacob Richardson, William Quinn, and Thomas Webster.[23] According to the journal of that date:

> *It was moved by Jacob Matthews, and seconded by Abner Coker, that Don Carlos Hall be appointed as a judge with the Bishop in time of election. It was put to voted, and carried, that the person that should be elected for an assistant to the General Superintendent should be voted for by private election, and the name of the person that should gain the election should be sealed up, and for to be kept in secret until after the Conference in Philadelphia has given their vote, and according to the Bishop's proposal, for him then to be set apart, if the two Conferences, Baltimore and Philadelphia, wished for it to be done, voted, and carried.*
>
> *It is a curious paper, showing a very awkward and contradictory movement, at least in the step toward making a second Bishop; but it was a first experience, in which two Conferences instead of one were concerned, and the authority vested in each body does not seem to be very clearly understood, stated, or acted upon.*

The Philadelphia Conference was not then in session, but in the election held in Baltimore, Morris Brown, Henry Harden, and Jacob Matthews were candidates, and the vote stood: Morris Brown, 7; Jacob Matthews, 9; Henry Harden, 4. The following month the Philadelphia Conference convened the 20th day of May, and we find the same three again as candidates for general superintendent, with the following result: Morris Brown, 9; Jacob Matthews, 15; Henry Harden, 9. The total vote stood: Morris Brown, 16; Jacob Matthews, 24; Henry Harden, 13.

For the first time Bishop Allen's name appears at the end of the Baltimore proceedings, and also in attestation of the genuineness of the electoral votes cast, both in Baltimore and Philadelphia, for the Episcopal assistant. The character and constitutionality of this election will be examined at another point. In this instance we have an evidence that election to the Episcopal office does not constitute any person a Bishop. "The laying on of hands" must follow election in order that the individual may be a veritable Bishop.[24]

CHAPTER V

MORRIS BROWN BECOMES THE SECOND BISHOP OF THE AME CHURCH

On May 25, 1828, Morris Brown was elected and consecrated the Second Bishop (and Allen's assumed successor) at the denomination's General Conference. He was later appointed to preside over the Bristol Circuit, Bucks County, in Philadelphia. He traveled extensively to establish new congregations and conferences. Brown and Allen worked closely together in Philadelphia and on a national level. Two issues that swept the AME Church were: 1) whether to suppress the efforts of the American Colonization Society (ACS); and 2) support for the abolitionist movement.

The American Colonization Society was formed in 1817 to send free blacks to Africa as an alternative to emancipation in the United States. In 1822, the society established on the west coast of Africa a colony that in 1847 became the independent nation of Liberia.

Regarding the abolitionist movement, a black abolitionist preacher, David Walker, wrote *An Appeal to the Coloured Citizens of the World*, which was a challenge to the forces of slavery and those who tolerated it. Walker published the *Appeal* in four articles. Walker's goal was to get blacks and whites to resist slavery while advocating for slaves to use physical rebellion. News about Walker's *Appeal* spread rapidly in the southern slaveholding states so that the governors of Virginia and South Carolina requested charges be brought against Walker and that he be arrested.

Both Allen and Brown supported Walker's writings claiming it was a religious document with scriptural references to the American Christian Church. They worked together in secrecy to encourage others to support the *Appeal*. Unfortunately, Walker later mysteriously died. Many assumed that he had been poisoned, while some believed he may have succumbed to tuberculosis, which had also killed his daughter

After Walker's death, Richard Allen called for a national convention of black people in Philadelphia on September 15, 1830. This national convention was to cut across all lines and was to include not only black churchmen, but blacks from all walks and political substructures for the first time in resistance to slavery and oppression. The 1830 convention, which historically is alluded to as the first National Black Congress, accomplished two major goals: 1) an agreement to suppress the efforts of the American Colonization Society; and, 2) an agreement to reaffirm its position in support of the ideology within David Walker's *Appeal*.

At Hillsboro, Ohio in August 1830, Brown organized the denomination's western churches (15 ministers and 1194 communicants, all in the territory between the Allegheny Mountains and the Mississippi River) into the Western (later Pittsburgh) Conference. Limited evangelization could be done in the south because even free blacks could be captured and sold into slavery. The African Church (which later became the

AME Church) had reopened in Charleston, only to be closed in 1834 as South Carolina banned all black churches in the aftermath of Nat Turner's slave rebellion in Virginia; thus the congregation was forced to meet secretly until after the Civil War.

After Ohio began enforcing notorious Black Codes in 1829, and other states (including Pennsylvania in 1838) followed suit, many blacks moved farther north, some to Canada. Bishop Brown organized the Canada Conference in Toronto in July 1840. The General Conference that year also assigned two missionaries: Elder N. Cannon to New England and Elder William Paul Quinn to the West. Growth within the latter also allowed its division—The Indiana Conference was established at Blue River in October 1840 and Elder Quinn was assigned to supervise both parts of the former western conferences. At the May 1844 General Conference, Elder Quinn reported that he had established 47 churches with 2000 members (including, daringly, one each in the slave territories of Louisville, Kentucky and St. Louis, Missouri assisted by 20 traveling and 27 local preachers. Fifty Sunday schools had also been organized (with 2000 students), as well as forty temperance societies and 17 camp meetings.

Allen worked arduously to develop a political format that would not be encumbered by the church. Mother Bethel had been operating as a fugitive slave center and Richard Allen encouraged other AME churches in strategic areas to do the same. However, the rigor and strain on Richard Allen's heart proved to be too much and he passed away in May of 1831. Allen's faithful protégé, Morris Brown, preached the funeral sermon on May 5th.

Allen's death occurred so close to the convening of the 1831 Annual Conference that the group considered postponing the conference. However, with significant business of the church to be considered while still in mourning, the AME Church convened in Philadelphia on May 21st. Bishop Morris Brown, considered to be black Methodism's "second in command" at the time, was overwhelmingly elected to chair the Conference. Assuming the mantle of Allen, Brown proceeded to fulfill Allen's vision urging the church to continue in its opposition to slavery.

Finding a successor to Allen as Presiding Bishop of the AME Church was to be decided before the conference adjourned. Brown's ability to lead was never in doubt. His administrative capabilities were known through his early work with the African Church of Charleston and through his ability to organize new districts and churches. Thus, it was no surprise when Brown was appointed as the Episcopal successor to Richard Allen. His association with Denmark Vesey and the Charleston insurrection made Brown immensely popular. Thus, when Bishop Richard Allen died in 1831, Brown took over the pastorate at AME Bethel Church and was elected and consecrated the Senior Bishop of the AME Church.

CHAPTER VI

MORRIS BROWN BECOMES THE SENIOR BISHOP OF THE AME CHURCH

As the senior bishop of the AME Church, Morris Brown traveled extensively, expanding the church from its northeastern base westward. His authority also extended southward to the church's missionary station in Haiti. During Brown's service as senior bishop, the denominational membership doubled to more than 17,000.

The original AME denomination was founded as The Free African Society in a blacksmith shop. The geographical spread of the African Methodist Episcopal Church prior to the Civil War was mainly restricted to the Northeast and Midwest. Major congregations were established in Philadelphia, New York, Boston, Pittsburgh, Baltimore, Washington, DC, Cincinnati, Chicago, Detroit, and other large cities. Remarkably, the slave states of Maryland, Kentucky, Missouri, Louisiana, and, for a few years, South Carolina, became additional locations for AME congregations.

In 1832, the Fourth General Conference of the AME Church convened in Philadelphia with Bishop Morris Brown presiding. One important issue to be addressed by the Conference attendees was the re-admission of Rev. William Paul Quinn to membership in the Church—Quinn had withdrawn from the AME Church to organize an Independent Methodist Church in New York City.[25] Another matter that Bishop Brown had to address was preventing ministers from non-slave holding states from going into Delaware—a slave state—to take charge of churches. Ultimately, all the appointments going into Delaware were changed and preachers were sent to conferences in other states. Rev. William Paul Quinn's application for readmission was granted; and following the General Conference, Brown organized the Western Conference at Pittsburg, where Rev. Quinn was immediately transferred. When the Western Conference met in Pittsburg with Bishop Brown presiding, the following anti-slavery resolution was passed:

> We, the members of this Conference, are fully satisfied that the principles of the Gospel are arrayed against sin, and that it is the duty of all Christians to use their influence and energies against all systems that rudely trample underfoot the claims of justice and the sacred principles of revelation. And
>
> Whereas, Slavery pollutes the character of the Church of God, and makes the Bible a sealed book to thousands of immortal beings, therefore, Resolved, that we will aid by our prayers, those pious persons whom God has raised up to plead the cause of the dumb, until every fetter shall be broken, and all men enjoy the liberty which the Gospel proclaims.[26]

Later, the Baltimore Conference opened with Bishop Morris Brown presiding, and Rev. Edward Waters acting as assistant to the Bishop. Rev. Levin Lee was elected secretary.

Nonetheless, the Baltimore AME Conference thrived, three AME churches had been founded in Virginia before the Civil War, and New Orleans also requested a traveling evangelist from the General Conference.

By 1840 at the Sixth General Conference, Brown had organized two new conferences—The Upper Canada and Indiana Conferences respectively. It was in the City of Toronto that Bishop Morris Brown called together the ministers and representatives of Methodism in Upper Canada, which was composed of twelve members.[27] Bishop Brown was assisted in the organization by Rev. Edmund Crosby, missionary for Canada, and Deacon George Ware of Rochester, New York. The Indiana Conference was organized at Blue River where Bishop Brown presided, and Major J. Wilkerson was selected as his assistant in the absence of Bishop Waters.

Not only was Brown a leader in the AME Church, but he also led in Philadelphia's American Moral Reform Society, an African American organization advocating anti-slavery, racial integration, and a myriad of other social reforms.

In 1842, the Canadian Conference territory was enlarged by adding Detroit, Michigan, and Queensbush, in the township of Peel, Canada West. The following month the Indiana Conference met for eight days on "the condition and prospect of the work committed to their care by God." Bishop Brown presided, assisted by William Paul Quinn—a highly regarded member of the church—for his work in planting the Western Missions which included eight circuits and stations, [and] a membership of 900, embracing a [black] community of 14,000 souls.[28]

Chapter VII

MORRIS BROWN'S LATER YEARS

While in Canada presiding at that Annual Conference in 1844, Brown suffered a stroke, which affected him the rest of his life leaving him partially paralyzed. The Philadelphia Conference granted him a $200 per year pension in 1845, and he continued as active in church affairs as his health permitted.

Aware that his own limited literacy affected his preaching, Brown mentored Daniel Payne, who had moved to Pennsylvania from Charleston after authorities closed his school in 1835. Although largely illiterate, Brown promoted education among clergy and lay members, whom he encouraged to attend schools where available. His focus was always education and temperance. When his fellow Charlestonian, Daniel Payne, joined the AME ministry in 1842, Brown encouraged his efforts to improve clerical education. So Payne studied at the Lutheran seminary in Gettysburg, but was not able to finish all four years at the seminary because of trouble with his eye that was caused by observing a solar eclipse.[29] Payne sustained the injury when he lived in South Carolina; but the damaged eye flared up again while he was in Gettysburg. But the education he received was significant for Payne because while he was at Gettysburg, he realized that his future vocation would be in the ordained ministry. In a diary entry after his accident, Payne wrote that his realization about the ministry came while he was lying on a bed, pondering his future. A voice inside of him (as if from God) screamed out "Woe is me if I preach not the Gospel!"[30] From that moment on, Payne was convinced that he should preach for the rest of his life. His two years at Gettysburg were a steppingstone for Payne, preparing him for the contribution that he would make later in life. At the General Conference of 1844, Brown helped Payne secure the adoption of a resolution requiring a regular course of study for ministers. Payne became the denomination's first historiographer in 1848.

Bishop Brown died in Philadelphia on May 9, 1849, having helped expand his denomination to include six conferences, 62 elders, nearly 300 churches and more than 17,000 members.[31] His protégé, Rev. Payne, delivered the eulogy. Originally buried in the former Mother Bethel Burying Ground, Morris Brown is now interred together with Bishop Richard Allen within the Mother Bethel Church.

After Bishop Brown's death, the denomination reached the Pacific Coast in the early 1850's with churches in Stockton, Sacramento, San Francisco, and other places in California. Moreover, Bishop Morris Brown previously established the Canada Annual Conference in 1840.

The most significant era of denominational development occurred during the Civil War and Reconstruction. Oftentimes, with the permission of Union army officials AME clergy moved into the states of the collapsing Confederacy to pull newly freed slaves into their denomination. "I Seek My Brethren", the title of an often-repeated sermon that Theophilus G.

Steward preached in South Carolina, became a clarion call to evangelize fellow blacks in Georgia, Florida, Alabama, Texas, and many other parts of the south. Hence, in 1880 AME membership reached 400,000 because of its rapid spread below the Mason-Dixon Line. When Bishop Henry M. Turner pushed African Methodism across the Atlantic into Liberia and Sierra Leone in 1891 and into South Africa in 1896, the AME now laid claim to adherents on two continents.

While the AME Church is doctrinally Methodist, clergy, scholars, and lay persons have written important works which demonstrate the distinctive theology and praxis which have defined this Wesleyan body. AME Bishop Benjamin W. Arnett, in an address to the 1893 World's Parliament of Religions, reminded the audience of the presence of blacks in the formation of Christianity. Bishop Benjamin T. Tanner wrote in 1895 in "The Color of Solomon—What?" that biblical scholars wrongly portrayed the son of David as a white man. In the post-civil rights era theologians James H. Cone, Cecil W. Cone, and Jacqueline Grant who came out of the AME tradition critiqued Euro-centric Christianity and African American churches for their shortcomings in fully impacting the plight of those oppressed by racism, sexism, and economic disadvantage.

After the American Civil War, Rev. Richard Harvey Cain of Charleston's African Church bought a Lutheran church building whose congregation had diminished by 1866, and the following year established the Morris Brown AME Church (becoming its first pastor). Furthermore, one of the first institutions of higher learning in the South, Morris Brown College in Atlanta, established in 1885 by the North Georgia Conference of the African Methodist Episcopal Church, was named after Bishop Brown.

Although Bishop Brown was deceased, his Episcopal tenure fanned the flames of liberation. AME clergy and laity were active in the movement to abolish slavery, and the *Christian Recorder* made literary and theological arguments for emancipation that prodded America's conscience. Under Brown's leadership, the AME Church made a significant impact on social justice issues that plagued the slaves and the free community daily.

RESOURCES

Brown's Opening Sermon

Preached Before the Baltimore Annual Conference of the African Methodist Episcopal Church, Held in Washington D.C.

> Hebrews xi. 24, 25. *"By faith Moses, when he was to come to years, refused to be called the son of Pharaoh's daughter; choosing rather to suffer affliction with the people of God than to enjoy the pleasures of sin for a season."*

While I endeavor to speak to you this morning, my dear brethren and sisters, I beg an interest in your prayers that God's blessing may rest upon my labors; for I intend to speak as the Lord may give me power. My labors have been great and tedious at the General Conference, so as to fatigue me very much; in addition to this, I took a cold on my way home, so that I don't feel able to speak to you very long this morning. And in these late years I have not been accustomed to divide and subdivide my subjects. I will speak in all simplicity and plainness of speech. We discover in the words selected for this morning's meditation, my brethren, that Moses, when he came to manhood, preferred suffering affliction with the people of God than to enjoy the pleasures of sin. So, we all ought to take his example—forsake the pleasures of the world and choose God as our rich inheritance.

We discover, my brethren, that God led Moses through all

his life, and made friends for him, even among those who had been the enemies of his injured people. For when his mother took and laid him in the bulrushes, and placed him upon the river's bank, among the flags, she never thought that her babe would find protection from the family of the king's daughter. She sent her maid to fetch it to her: the tears falling from his little eyes created a mother's feeling for the helpless infant. Then said the sister of Moses, "Shall I go and call to thee a nurse of the Hebrew women, that she may nurse the child for thee?" And Pharaoh's daughter said, "Go." So, she went and called the mother of Moses, and Pharaoh's daughter said unto her. "Take this child away and nurse it for me, and I will give thee thy wages." And when the child grew, she carried it to the princess, and he became her son, and she caused him to be educated in all the arts and sciences of the Egyptians. No doubt, my brethren, that from the earliest period of his life his mind was impressed with a great sympathy for his afflicted people. And it must not be supposed that he was without enemies; for, like Joseph, his standing and the peculiar love which the royal family bestowed upon him, must have excited the envy of his neighbors; for those who are useful and men of talents are always disliked by narrow-hearted persons. It will be recollected that the Children of Israel were led into Egypt by a mysterious providence. Joseph, the favorite son of Israel, for whom was made a coat of many colors, was hated by his brethren, and by them was sold into Egypt; and notwithstanding he was by this circumstance placed in a very mean condition, yet so great was his piety that the favor of God rested continually upon him, which caused him to increase in popularity and esteem with the king so that he soon became the greatest man in the nation.

In the midst of his power a universal famine caused his brethren and aged father to remove from the land of Egypt, where they were fed and protected by the authority of the king. The services of Joseph secured his family and immediate posterity, and that of his brethren, the favor of the government of Egypt; but in process of time his greatness and goodness were forgotten, and the hapless Israelites were cruelly oppressed until Moses, who had become of age, was walking abroad one day, and seeing an Egyptian oppressing one of his people, drew near and slew him. The next day he saw two of his brethren contending with each other, and when he went to make peace, one of them charged him with having slain the Egyptian, which caused him to be afraid, so that he fled into the land of Midian, and was there until God sent him to deliver his afflicted people.

To make a practical use of the text, we say that but few, my brethren, make a choice as wise as that of Moses. For we discover that, although many profess to have forsaken the world and suffer affliction with the children of God, they know but little about his love. They have the form but not the power of godliness; for they will envy and backbite their brethren. It was not so with Moses; for we will discover, my brethren, that he set his whole heart upon God. His heart was in heaven because his treasures were there; for where the treasure is there will the heart be also. Many desire to serve God, but their hearts are upon the world, upon its riches, or honors, or its lusts. I knew a man in Charleston, S.C., who, if he is alive, is about eighty years of age. He was a slave, but he was also a man of prayer; and he used to go with me on a Saturday night to preach the Gospel to the slaves on the plantations in South Carolina. One day he said: "If I should be a free man, I will give half my time to God, the other half to my business." Sometime after his master died and left him free. A short while after this I called on him to go and help me preach. He excused himself by saying if he left his work the people who patronized him would complain and say that he neglected his business. About six months after I called again to get his labors, but he was so full of business he could not go. I went again the third time, but he was making too much money to leave his business. I only tell this to show how few will give up the world for God like Moses. Nothing, my friends, could charm him of an earthly character. He was determined to glorify his God, and so it is with the man whose heart is set upon heaven; he will let nothing happen to him from doing his duty. No trouble, no crosses, no persecution can hinder him; and so it was in the days of Peter, when he wrote his General Epistle to strengthen his Hebrew brethren under the persecution of the Heathen Romans. So, I exhort you, my brethren, to let nothing keep you from your duty to God, neither persecution, poverty, nor affliction. Oh, let your hearts be in heaven, and God will be with you by night and by day; but if you grow weary and doubt by the way, he will forsake you and let you go by yourself; for none get to the kingdom or get his protection, my brethren, whose trust is not in him. O, then, my brethren, strive to live for God. As the apostle saith, faith, hope and charity, but the greatest of these is charity—have charity, then, or love for God, and he will give you grace to meet all things. Yes, my brethren, where faith and hope shall fail, charity will bear you through the gates of death and triumph.

In this unfriendly world he will be with you as he is with our dear brother Richard Williams, who died last week in the triumphs of faith, and is now singing doxologies with the saints and angels in heaven. Let his example encourage you, and then, like Paul, you will be able to say: "I have fought the good fight, I have kept the faith, I have finished my course; henceforth, there is a crown laid up for me which the Righteous Judge shall give me in that day."[32]

Brown's Last Will and Testament

Bishop Morris Brown's will was enforced on May 9, 1849 when he expired this life and made his eternal departure. His death was consequential to his suffering a stroke while in Canada attending to Episcopal business, thus he was bedridden for five years. Bishop Morris Brown was uneducated; therefore, he used an 'X' to sign his name in order to legitimize his will.

In his will he bequeathed the following: that his house and lot situated on Queen Street between 4th and 5th, Philadelphia, be sold to help pay his debts and the balance to be towards supporting his wife, Maria Brown, and his three children, named: Samuel, Martha, and Charlotte. He bequeathed to his wife, Maria during her widowhood his house and lot on shipped Street between 7th and 8th streets, and all of his household goods and kitchen furniture, and in case of her discontinuance of her widowhood or death, to his three youngest children via—Samuel, Martha, and Charlotte. To his son, Samuel Brown he left, all his wearing apparels and the four volumes of Patrick Lowth's "Commentary on the Old and New Testament": to his son, Malcolm Brown he bequeathed his "History of the Church" and one volume of Burrkitt's "Works." He gave to his wife Maria all the balance of his books.

Morris Brown's last will and testament tells a lot of his character as a man. It shows that he was highly responsible, for the well-being of his family was paramount. Consequently, he planned toward the future to ensure that his family's welfare remain intact even in the event of his death. Furthermore, he seemed to have been a good steward of the blessings of God based on the accumulation of his earthly possessions. Therefore, his life is a testament that with hard work and dedication no mountain is insurmountable.[33]

NOTES

1   Yee, Morris Brown, https://www.blackpast.org/
    african-american-history/brown-morris-1770-1849

2   Claudia Sutherland. 2018. "Stono Rebellion (1739)" *Black-
    past,* https://www.blackpast.org/african-american-history/
    stono-rebellion-1739/

3   Mark R. Jones, *Wicked Charleston: The Dark side of the Holy City*
    (Charleston: The History Press, 2005), 88.

4   John 1:29 KJV

5   Bartlett, Brown Fellowship Society (1790–1945),
    https://www.blackpast.org/african-american-history/
    brown-fellowship-society-1790-1945/

6   Jones, *Wicked Charleston*: 88.

7   Yee, Morris Brown, https://www.blackpast.org/
    african-american-history/brown-morris-1770-1849

8   Egerton, *Brown, Morris*. Encyclopedia of African American Histo-
    ry, 1619-1895, http://www.oxfordaasc.com/article/print/opr/0004/
    e0084?image_size=inline, 82.

9   Chicora Foundation, Inc., History of African American Cemeteries,
    (South Carolina: SCIWAY.net, LLC, 1996) https://www.sciway.net/
    hist/chicora/gravematters.html.

10 Laurie F. Maffly-Kipp. (2001). An Introduction to the Church in
    the Southern Black Community Documenting the American South.
    University Library, The University of North Carolina at Chapel Hill,
    (2001) https://docsouth.unc.edu/church/intro.html

11 John M. Lofton, "Denmark Vesey's Call to Arms," Journal of Negro
    History 33, no. 1 (1948): 404.

12 Thomas Gale Denmark Vesey (1767-1822). Black History; Biogra-
    phies. www.cbn.com/special/blackhistory/bio_denmark_vesey.aspx

13 Egerton, He Shall Go Out Free: The Lives of Denmark Vesey, 16-23

14 Egerton, And He Shall Go Out Free, 122

15 Egerton, And He Shall Go Out Free, 121; see also Sarah Silverman & Lewis Walker eds., A Documented History of Gullah Jack Pritchard and the Denmark Vesey Slave Insurrection of 1822, (Lewiston: E. Mellen Press, 2000), 95-97.

16 Denmark Vesey: This Far By Faith. https://www.pbs.org/thisfarby-faith/people/denmark_vesey.html

17 Kat Chow, "Denmark Vesey And The History Of Charleston's 'Mother Emanuel' Church," NPR Code Switch: Race & Identity Remixed, June 18, 2015, https://www.npr.org/sections/codeswitch/2015/06/18/415465656/denmark-vesey-and-the-history-of-charleston-s-mother-emanuel-church

18 Albert J. Raboteau, Slave Religion: The Invisible Institution in the Antebellum South, (Oxford University Press, 2004), 163.

19 Lofton, "Denmark Vesey's Call to Arms," 412-413.

20 Thomas W. Higginson, "The Story of Denmark Vesey," The Atlantic, June, 1861.

21 Denmark Vesey: This Far By Faith. https://www.pbs.org/thisfarby-faith/people/denmark_vesey.html; see also, Saillant, John. "Before 1822: Anti-Black Attacks on Charleston Methodist Churches from 1786 to Denmark Vesey's Execution." Common-place.org. 16, no. 2 (Winter 2016). http://common-place.org/book/before-1822-anti-black-attacks-on-charleston-methodist-churches-from-1786-to-denmark-veseys-execution/.

22 Richard Newman, Freedom's Prophet: Bishop Richard Allen, the AME Church, and the Black Founding Fathers. (New York: New York University Press 2008).

23 Daniel A. Payne, D.D., LL.D: History of the African Methodist Episcopal Church (Nashville, Tenn.: Publishing House of the A. M. E. Sunday School Union, 1891).

24 Payne, History of the African Methodist Episcopal Church, 22-23

25 James Handy, Scraps of the AME Church, (Philadelphia: A.M.E. Book Concern, (1902).

26 Handy, Scraps of the AME Church, 141

27 Handy, Scraps of the AME Church, 138

28 Handy, Scraps of the AME Church, 149-150

29 Vazzano, Brian A., The Life and Impact of Daniel Alexander Payne (2006). Hidden in Plain Sight Projects. https://cupola.gettysburg.edu/hiddenpapers/36

30 Vazzano, The Life and Impact of Daniel Payne.

31 Handy, Scraps of the AME Church.

32 Handy, Scraps of the AME Church.

33 Handy, Scraps of the AME Church.

BIBLIOGRAPHY

Aaseng, Nathan. (2011). "Brown, Morris." In African-American Religious Leaders, Revised Edition, A to Z of African Americans, edited by Nathan Aaseng. New York: Facts on File, Inc., 2011.

Adams, Sr, Eugene Avery. Yearbook and Historical Guide to the African Methodist Episcopal Church. Columbia, South Carolina: Bureau of Research and History, 1955.

Africans in America. "The Vesey Conspiracy: 1822. Brotherly Love, Part 3: (1791-1831). Accessed 2014. www.pbs.org/wgbh/aia/part3/3p2976.html.

African American Heritage. Voices: Stories of Change, Charleston: SC. Historical Timeline. Accessed 2014. https://www.africanamericancharleston.com/timeline/.

Allen, Richard, and Jacob Tapisco. 1817. The Doctrines and Disciplines of the African Methodist Episcopal Church. Documenting the American South. University Library, The University of North Carolina at Chapel Hill, 2001. www.docsouth.unc.edu/church/ame/ame.html.

Allen, Richard. 1833. The Life, Experience, and Gospel Labours of the Rt. Rev. Richard Allen. Documenting the American South. University Library, The University of North Carolina at Chapel Hill, 2000. https://docsouth.unc.edu/neh/allen/menu.html.

Allen Richard. "Eulogy of George Washington," delivered in Bethel Church December 29, 1799, and reprinted in the Philadelphia Gazette, December 31, 1799. In "We Participate in Common": Richard Allen's Eulogy of Washington and the Challenge of Interracial Appeals by Richard S. Newman. William and Mary Quarterly 64, No. 1 (January 2007): 117-128. Accessed 2014, The President's House in Philadelphia. http://www.ushistory.org/presidentshouse/history/alleneulogy.php.

AME Church: 7th Episcopal District. Our History, from 7th District AME Church, South Carolina: Accessed 2014. https://ame7.church/our-history/.

Asbury, Francis. Journal of Rev. Francis Asbury, Bishop of the Methodist Episcopal Church. Volume III. New York: Lane & Scott, 1852.

Barnes, Sandra. L. "Priestly and Prophetic Influences on Black Church Social Services." Social Problems 51, no. 2 (May 2004): 202-221.

Barnes, Sandra. L. "Black Church Culture and Community Action." Social Forces 84, no. 2 (December 2005): 967-994.

Bartlett, Sarah. "Brown Fellowship Society (1790-1945)." BlackPast, September 14, 2010. www.blackpast.org/aah/brown-fellowship-society-1790-1945/.

Birnie, C. W. "Education of the Negro in Charleston, South Carolina, Prior to the Civil War." The Journal of Negro History 12, no. 1 (1927): 13-21. http://www.jstor.org/stable/2714159.

Black History in America. "Denmark Vesey." Accessed 2014. www.myblackhistory.net/Denmark_Vesey.htm.

Cannon, Noah Calwell W. 1842. A History of the African Methodist Episcopal Church, the Only One in the United States of America, Styled Bethel Church (Gen. xxviii.19.): To be Held Forth in Remembrance of the Right Reverend Richard Allen, First Bishop of the Connection: Electronic Ed. Documenting the American South. University Library, The University of North Carolina at Chapel Hill, 2000. www.docsouth.unc.edu/church/cannon/cannon.html.

Dickerson, Dennis. C. "Our History." The Official Website African Methodist Episcopal Church. Accessed 2014. www.ame-church.com/our-church/our-history.

Documenting the American South. About Documenting the American South. University Library, The University of North Carolina at Chapel Hill. Accessed 2014. https://docsouth.unc.edu/support/about/.

Egerton, Douglas R. He Shall Go Out Free: The Lives of Denmark Vesey / Edition 1. Lanham, Maryland: Rowman & Littlefield Publishers, Inc. 2000.

Egerton, Douglas R. Judging the Founders: Richard Allen and the Soul of America. Reviews in American History 37, no. 1 (March 2009): 22-27.

Egerton, Douglas R. "Brown, Morris." In Encyclopedia of African American History, 1619-1895: From the Colonial Period to the Age of Frederick Douglass, edited by Paul. Finkelman, Vol I. Oxford University Press, 2009. Accessed April 2014. http://www.oxfordaasc.com/article/print/opr/0004/e0084?image_size=inline.

Ellison, C. G., & D. E. Sherkat, "The 'Semi-involuntary Institution' Revisited: Regional Variations in Church Participation among Black Americans." Social Forces 73, no. 4, (June 1995):1415-1437.

Emanuel A.M.E. Church. National Park Service: Accessed 2014. https://www.nps.gov/places/emanuel-a-m-e-church.htm.

Emanuel African Methodist Episcopal Church. "Mother Emanuel" A.M.E. Church History. (July 11, 2014). Emanuel African Methodist Episcopal Church. Accessed 2014. www.emanuelamechurch. org/churchhistory.php.

Fitchett, E. H. "The Traditions of the Free Negro in Charleston, South Carolina." The Journal of Negro History 25, no. 2, (April 1940): 139-152. Accessed 2014. http://www.jstor.org/ stable/2714595.

Fitchett, E. H. "The Origin and Growth of the Free Negro Population of Charleston, South Carolina." The Journal of Negro History, 26, no. 4, (October 1941): 421-437. Accessed 2014. http://www. jstor.org/stable/2715006.

Fitchett, E. H. "The Status of the Free Negro in Charleston, South Carolina, and His Descendants in Modern Society: Statement of the Problem." The Journal of Negro History 32, no. 4, (October 1947): 430-451. Accessed 2014. https://www.jstor.org/ stable/2714926.

Forbes, Robert P. "Recent Books on Denmark Vesey." The North Star: A Journal of African American Religious History 3, vol. 2, (Spring 2000). Accessed 2014. https://www.princeton.edu/~jweisenf/northstar/volume3/v3n2.html.

Ford, Frederick. A. 1861. Charleston (S.C.). City Council Census of the City of Charleston, South Carolina, for the Year 1861. Illustrated by Statistical Tables. Prepared under the Authority of the City Council by Frederick A. Ford. Documenting the American South. University Library, The University of North Carolina at Chapel Hill, 2000. https://docsouth.unc.edu/imls/census/census. html.

Gale, T. "Black History Biographies: Denmark Vesey (1767-1822)." Farmington, MI: 1999. Junior Reference Collection. CBN. Accessed 2014. www.cbn.com/special/blackhistory/bio_denmark_vesey.aspx.

Gatewood, Willard B. Aristocrats of Color: The Black Elite, 1880-1920. University of Arkansas Press, 2000.

Greene, Harlan, Harry. S. Hutchens, and Brian E. Hutchins. (2008). Slave Badges and the Slave-Hire System in Charleston, South Carolina, 1783-1865. Jefferson, North Carolina: McFarland & Company, Incorporated, 2004.

Gross, Robert A. "Forum: The Making of a Slave Conspiracy, part 1." The William and Mary Quarterly 58, no. 4, (October 2001): 913-914. Accessed 2014. https://www.jstor.or/stable/2674505?-read-now=1&refreqid=exce,sior3A16cOaabe390617fc1b3948c0f5153a5f&seq=1#page_scan_tab_contents.

Hamilton, James. 1822. Negro Plot. An Account of the Late Intended Insurrection among a Portion of the Blacks of the City of Charleston, South Carolina: Electronic Edition. Documenting the American South. University Library, The University of North Carolina at Chapel Hill, 1999. Accessed 2014. www.docsouth.unc.edu/church/hamilton/hamilton.html.

Handy, James. A. 1902. Scraps of African Methodist Episcopal History: Electronic Edition. Documenting the American South. University Library, The University of North Carolina at Chapel Hill, 1999. Accessed 2014. www.docsouth.unc.edu/church/handy/handy.html.

Higginson, Thomas Wentworth. "The Story of Denmark Vesey." The Atlantic, June, 1861.

Johnson, Michael P. "Denmark Vesey and His Co-Conspirators." The William and Mary Quarterly 58, no. 4, (October 2001): 915-976. Accessed 2014. http://www.jstor.org/stable/2674506.

Johnson, W. D. (1892, April). "Educational Work of the African M.E. Church: History of the AME Church." African Methodist Episcopal Church Review 8, no. 4 (April 1892): 391-399. Ohio Historical Society: The African-American Experience in Ohio (1850-1920). Accessed 2014. http://dbs.ohiohistory.org/africanam/html/nwspaper/.

Jones, Lewis P. "South Carolina." In Religion in the Southern States: A Historical Study, edited by Samuel S. Hill, 263-288. Macon: Mercer University Press, 1983. Accessed 2014. https://books.google.com/books?id=8YglsnWiXJYC&pg=PP9&source=gbs_selected_pages&cad=2#v=onepage&q&f=false.

Lofton, John M. "Denmark Vesey's Call to Arms." The Journal of Negro History 33, no. 4 (1948): 395-417. doi:10.2307/2715918.

Morgan, Philip D. "Conspiracy Scares." The William and Mary Quarterly 59, no. 1 (January 2002): 159-166. http://www.jstor.org/stable/3491645.

Nell, W. C., Downing, G. T., & W.W. Brown. "Letters to Antislavery Workers and Agencies (Part 8)." The Journal of Negro History 10, no. 3 (July 1925): 519-543.

Newman, A. (1844). "The Rev. Morris Brown of Philadelphia." National Portrait Gallery Collection. 1844. Smithsonian Institution. Accessed July 2014. collections.si.edu/search/record/npg_NPG.99.94.

Newman, Richard. S. Freedom's Prophet. New York: NYU Press, 2009.

NNDB. Robert Purvis. NNDB: Tracking the Entire World. Accessed 2014. https://www.nndb.com/people/968/000172452/.

Okur, Nilgun Anadolu. "Underground Railroad in Philadelphia." Journal of Black Studies, 25, no. 5 (May 1995): 537-557. Accessed 2014. http://www.jstor.org/stable/2784630.

Paquette, R. L. "Review." Review of Slave Badges and the Slave-Hire System in Charleston, South Carolina, 1783-1865, by Harlan Greene and Harry S. Hutchins. The South Carolina Historical Magazine, 107, no. 1 (January 2006): 44-47. Accessed 2014. http://www.jstor.org/stable/27570789.

Payne, Daniel. 1891. History of the African Methodist Episcopal Church: Electronic Edition. (C. Spencer, Editor) Documenting the American South. University Library, The University of North Carolina at Chapel Hill, 2001. Accessed 2014. www.docsouth.unc.edu/church/payne/payne.html.

Pearson, Edward. 'Trials and Errors: Denmark Vesey and His Historians." The William and Mary Quarterly 59, no. 1 (January 2002): 137-142. Accessed 2014. http://www.jstor.org/stable/3491642.

Petrey, Whitney. Slaves in Revolutionary America: Plantation Slaves in Virginia and the Charleston Slave Trade. Academia. Accessed 2014. http://www.academia.edu/1701748/Slaves_in_Revolutionary_America_Plantation_Slaves_in_Virginia_and_the_Charleston_Slave_Trade.

Pohanka, Brian. (1863, July 18). "Fort Wagner and the 54th Massachusetts Volunteer Infantry." Civil War Trust, July 18, 1863. www.civilwar.org/battlefields/batterywagner/battery-wagner-history-articles/fortwagnerpohanka.html.

Rankin, John. "John Rankin Papers: Review of the Statement of the Faculty of Lane Seminary in Relation to the Recent Difficulties in that Institution." The Ohio Historical Society: The African-American Experience in Ohio (1850-1920) (1835). Accessed 2014. http://dbs.ohiohistory.org/africanam/html/pagec6ba.html?ID=2977&Current=F001&View=Text.

Reverdy C. Ransom Collection, 1906-1957. The Ohio Historical Society: The African-American Experience in Ohio (1850-1920). http://dbs.ohiohistory.org/africanam/html/mss/856.html.

Ripley (Ohio) Anti-Slavery Society Minute Book. (1838-1848). The Ohio Historical Society: The African-American Experience in Ohio 1850-1920. http://dbs.ohiohistory.org/africanam/html/page5e99.html?ID=13904&Current=035.

Robert, Richard (Richard R. Wright). 1816. Centennial Encyclopedia of the African Methodist Episcopal Church. Documenting the American South. University Library, The University of North Carolina at Chapel Hill. Accessed 2014. www.docsouth.unc.edu/church/wright/ill299a.html.

Rucker, Walter C. "I Will Gather All Nations": Resistance, Culture, and Pan-African Collaboration in Denmark Vesey's South Carolina." The Journal of Negro History 86, no. 2 (Spring 2001): 132-147. Accessed 2014. http://www.jstor.org/stable/1350161.

Ruffle, Karen. Noah Calwell W. Cannon 1796?-1850. Documenting the American South. University Library, The University of North Carolina at Chapel Hill. Accessed 2014. www.docsouth.unc.edu/church/cannon/bio.html.

Sidbury, James. "Plausible Stories and Varnished Truths." The William and Mary Quarterly 59, no.1 (January 2002): 179-184. Accessed 2014. http://www.jstor.org/stable/3491648.

Spencer, J. M. "The Hymnody of the African Methodist Episcopal Church." American Music 8, no. 3 (1990): 274-293. Accessed 2014.

Stroud, M. (2011, December 29). "Emanuel AME Church." The Historical Marker Database. (December 29, 2011) Accessed 2014. www.hmdb.org/marker.asp?marker=51900.

Sutherland, Claudia. "Denmark Vesey Conspiracy of 1822." Blackpast, March 27, 2007. www.blackpast.org/aah/denmark-vesey-conspiracy-1822.

Toplin, Robert. "Mulattoes, 1830-1861". The Journal of Southern History 45, no. 2 (May, 1979): 185-200. http://www.jstor.org/stable/2208151.

US Slave. "Emanuel AME Church of Charleston." US Slave, March 16, 2012. Accessed 2014. www.usslave.blogspot.com/2012/03/emanuel-ame-church-of-charleston.html.

Vazzano, Bryan. "The Life and Impact of Daniel Alexander Payne." Gettysburg College, Spring 2006. Hidden in Plain Sight Projects. 36. htps://cupola.gettysburg.edu/hiddenpapers/36.

Walker, J. S. (1972). "Morris Brown: Crisis Leadership of the African Methodist Episcopal Church—1830-1850." Perspective: Journal of Pittsburgh Theological Seminary 13, no. 2 (1972): 138-155.

William J. Barnett Manumission Papers: America Barnett Manumission Paper. (March 2, 1859). The Ohio Historical Society: The African American Experience in Ohio (1850-1920). http://dbs.ohiohistory.org/africanam/html/deted7c.html?ID=2979.

William J. Barnett Manumission Papers: Sam Barnett Manumission Paper. (March 2, 1859). The Ohio Historical Society: The African-American Experience in Ohio (1850-1920): http://dbs.ohiohistory.org/africanam/html/page9d8b.html?ID=2978&Current=01&View=Text.

Witnesses to Faith. Daniel Payne. This Far by Faith. Accessed 2014. www.pbs.org/thisfarbyfaith/people/daniel_payne.html.

Witnesses to Faith. Denmark Vesey. This Far by Faith. Accessed 2014. www.pbs.org/thisfarbyfaith/people/denmark_vesey.html.

Wright, Richard (Richard Robert). 1816. Centennial Encyclopedia of the African Methodist Episcopal Church. Documenting the American South. University Library, The University of North Carolina at Chapel Hill. Retrieved 2014. www.docsouth.unc.edu/church/wright/ill299a.html.

Yee, Shirley. "Morris Brown (1770-1849)." BlackPast. April 26, 2008. www.blackpast.org/aah/brown-morris-1770-1849.